OUT OF THE BOX

Dedicated to Robert Creeley

who wrote me

"Guys like us are always outsiders"

BASIL KING

SPUYTEN DUYVIL
New York City

A short story never ends

I never asked my mother or Aunt Jenny why they rented a house in a village that is 8 miles North-West of the town of Northampton?

Pause

In 1940 the village of Creaton maintained a church
with a low stone tower
built in the 12th century
A symbol of the past
redeems the present?
Had there been a murder?
something that wasn't
to be spoken about
Had cruelty been inflicted
Had incest and rape
ravaged the small community?
Ancient loyalty
Silenced the tongues

Pause

A horse trough on the village green supplied water
    to many of the cottages
They had tin or thatched roofs
The cottage we lived in had cold running water

Pause

We were called the foreigners by the locals

I was always fearful of my safety
in the village
but when I'd take the path
away from the village to fields
that had been farms
to tents where the enlisted men
were stationed
I would be welcomed

A number of the soldiers
were from London
they would come to our cottage
and have tea with my aunt and mother

The Manor House built in 1604
housed the officers

There was something surreal in that
it was gossiped that this regiment
was being trained to go to the desert
Here they were training in the green fields of England

Pause

Built onto one side of the church
The school room was one long
narrow room with a high ceiling
that always felt damp
The school had electricity
Three outhouses that always smelt
I sat in one of the front rows
with the younger children
Cousin Renee who is three or four years older than me
    sat towards the back

The teacher was a small
humorless woman
She sat on a stool
that never moved
Barking commands
and wielding
a long switch
that she used
on every student's
infraction

For the majority
of the village children
school was a daily imposition
The teacher had no enthusiasm
or interest in any of us
Her only interest
was correct answers
good behavior

Pause

Wanting to know more of
Creaton's history
I found
on the internet
Creaton was the birthplace
of Amphylis Twigden (1601-1655)
She was the great-great grandmother
of George Washington

In the center of the village
across Grooms Lane are the foundations of the house
    where Amphylis was born
Amphylis married Reverend Lawrence Washington (1602-1652)
He was a Don at Oxford and from 1632-1643
    was Rector of the wealthy
All Saints Church Purleigh in Essex

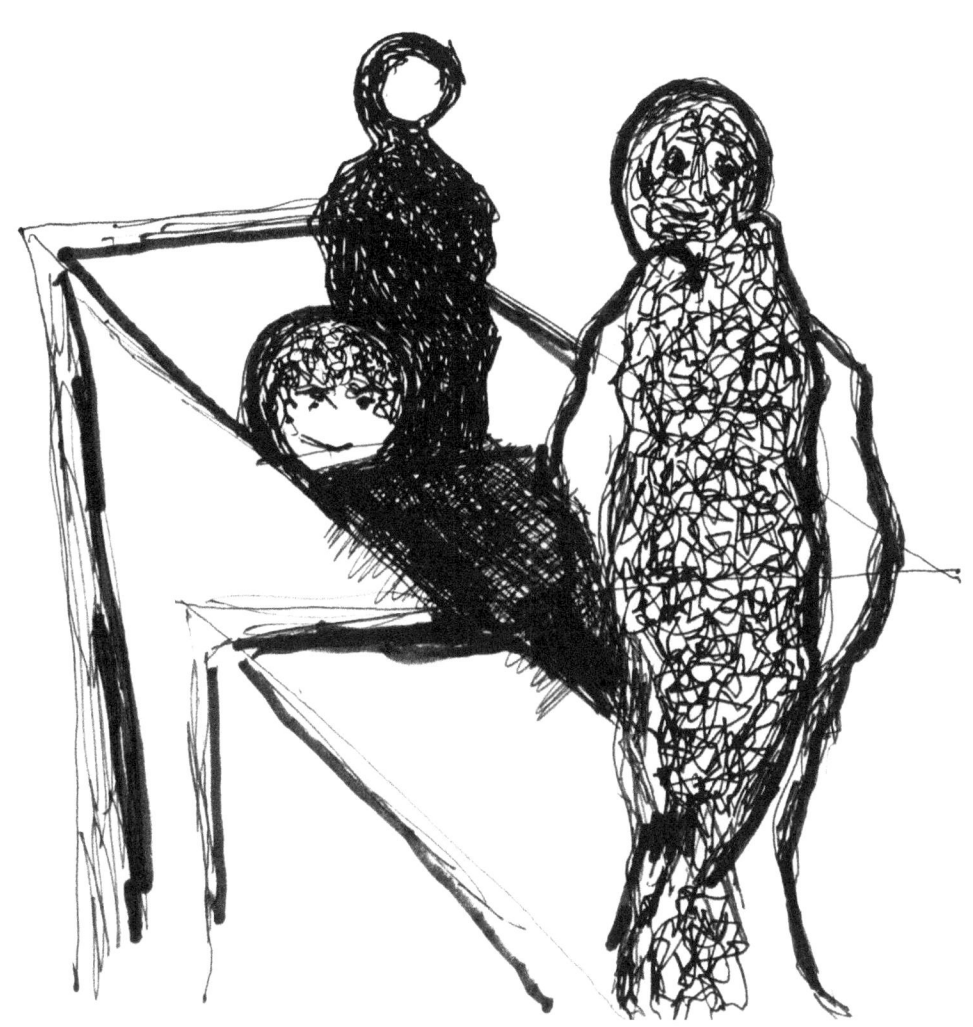

Lawrence married Amphylis in 1632
They had 6 children
In 1643 the Puritan Parliament
drummed him out of his position
on trumped up charges
of being "a common frequenter
of ale houses(encouraged) others
in that beastly vice"
He was sent to the impoverished parish of Braxton in Essex

Amphylis and the children
did not go with him
They were taken in
by a wealthy cousin
Sir Edwin Sandys
Lawrence spent
seven years
eking out an existence
died penniless and left no will

Pause

I was asked by the villagers
why do Jews
bury their dead standing up
They wanted to see my horns

Pause

My exit from Creaton was violent
For years I convinced myself
what happened was because
of anti-Semitism
but I was wrong
It was because
my mother had taught me
to read and write
before I was five
and I mocked the older boys
for their lack of
reading and writing skills
and they wanted to kill me

The boys dragged me
to the horse trough
held me down
dunked my head
time and again
into the water
I saw stars

and it became
life threatening
The dunking didn't stop
until my cousin Renee
stopped them

Pause

I woke up not knowing
how long I had
been in a hospital ward
with wounded soldiers
The soldiers were young men
with an arm missing
a leg
A number of them had bandages
around their faces
Nobody was blind
but a few were bedridden
They had books and magazines
played the radio
cards checkers and chess
I was a five year old
Without his parents
and every man
treated me with kindness

I'd developed a mastoid infection
from the dunking and was operated on
To this day when a doctor
looks in my ear
they want to know who operated
Whoever he was he was a master surgeon

Due to a shortage of nurses
one of the men
who must have been a medic
gave me shots
in my ear
as another man
held my shoulders down

Pause

There was a shortage of pajamas
One day we got tops
the following day
we got bottoms
If on a day when the men
were only wearing tops
and a nurse came to the ward
to change

one of the men's bandages
Every man's
erect penis was visible

On some occasions
if one of the men
came close to a nurse
the nurse would flick
her fingers against
his erect penis

It wasn't until
I became potent
did I become aware
of how painful
these encounters were
for the soldiers and the nurses

Pause

I don't know how long
I'd been in the hospital
when I was given a top
and a bottom
a dressing gown and slippers
Seated in a wheelchair
I was taken to a room
with a glass wall

On the other side of the glass wall stood my parents smiling and wav-
ing
I waved back
and a few minutes later
I was returned
to the ward
All the clothing
I had worn
was taken from me
 and I was given a top
A few days later
I was released
from the hospital
and went
with my parents
to a rooming house
where they were living

Pause

A short story never ends

The inhabitants of the village
were the offspring of farm workers
who worked for wealthy landed gentry
hundreds of years ago
And it is possible
The present day villagers
didn't know what had occurred
between their ancestors
between their masters
masters and their workers
But something diabolic had occurred that haunted generation
after generation of villagers
and it produced paranoia a mistrust
that constantly overwhelmed
life in the village

Too often I have told this story as if I was going to the store
    for a loaf of bread
When living in Creaton
was the first time
I got to know
I was an outsider

www.ingramcontent.com/pod-product-compliance
Lightning Source LLC
Chambersburg PA
CBHW041157120626
46547CB00020B/3246